Moral Support

A play by

William Considine

Finishing Line Press
Georgetown, Kentucky

Moral Support

To all who have lived and loved in troubled families

Copyright © 2025 by **William Considine**
ISBN 979-8-88838-935-5 First Edition
All rights reserved under International and Pan-American Copyright Conventions. No part of this book may be reproduced in any manner whatsoever without written permission from the publisher, except in the case of brief quotations embodied in critical articles and reviews.

Moral Support opened an eight-performance premiere production run at Medicine Show Theatre in New York City on February 21, 2019, directed by Félix Gardón, with the following cast:

Mike	……	Richard Keyser
Mary	……	Cynthia Shaw
Beth	……	Nora McCarthy
Father	……	David A. P. Brown
Older Mike	……	David A. P. Brown

Stage manager: Brie Mann-Hernandez
Costumer: Janet Mervin
Lighting designer: Patrick John Ashcroft.

Thank you to Chris Brandt, Rose-Marie Brandwein, Tyler Kent, Diane Tyler, Carla Torgrimson, John L Payne, Elinor Nauen, Martha King, Polaris North and Prose Pros.

All rights reserved. Persons wishing to stage *Moral Support* or a portion of it in any medium should contact the author at: wconsidinewritings@gmail.com

Publisher: Leah Huete de Maines
Editor: Christen Kincaid
Cover Art: Richard Keyser and Cynthia Shaw in performance at Medicine Show Theater, February 2019. Photograph by Fernando Natalici.
Author Photo: Careen Shannon
Cover Design: Elizabeth Maines McCleavy

Order online: www.finishinglinepress.com
   also available on amazon.com

Author inquiries and mail orders:
Finishing Line Press
PO Box 1626
Georgetown, Kentucky 40324
USA

Cast of Characters

Mike: A law student, age 24

Mary: His mother, age 46, ill with cancer, divorced, lives alone

Beth: Father's sister, age 58, an office worker, lives with Father

Father: Mike's father, also named Mike, age 48, a fireman and plumber

Older Mike: Mike 24 years later, a lawyer, played by the actor who also plays Father

Scene and Time

Scene 1: A declining steel city in 1972; Mary's apartment

Scene 2: The same city and year; Father's house

Scene 3: Father's house, remembered, in 1996

Scene 1

SETTING: The living room of MARY's apartment. Morning. A sofa, chairs and television. Stage left, doorway to the kitchen. Stage right, the door into the apartment, and the hallway. Rear center, the doorway into the bedroom.

AT RISE: MIKE *approaches the door, pauses, then knocks.*

MIKE
Mom… Mom… It's Mike…. Mom…

(*MARY comes quietly out of the bedroom and puts on a housecoat.*)

Mom… How are you? … I want to see you.

MARY
Mike?

MIKE
Hi.

MARY
Is that you?

MIKE
It's Mike, Mom. Yeh.

MARY
Are you alone?

MIKE
Yeh. I tried calling you. On the phone. You didn't answer.

MARY
I must have been sleeping. Wait a minute. I'll get the door.

MIKE
Great.

MARY
I'm not dressed. I mean, I've got a robe on. I wish I'd known you were coming.

MIKE
I called.

(MARY opens the door.)

MARY
Hello, stranger.

MIKE
Hey, Mom.

(MIKE embraces her.)

Hey, you look good. Really good. You gained weight.

MARY
Oh, I've got a belly you wouldn't believe. Look at this.

MIKE
It's good. It shows you're eating.

MARY
I don't have my wig on.

MIKE
The natural look.

MARY
No, no. Your mother wears a wig now. Just look at this.

(MARY indicates her hair.)

MIKE
Oh, it's fine. Lived in! Natural. How do you feel?

MARY
Pretty good. They say I've got a good spirit, and that's what counts. All the nurses think I'm a nut. I joke around a lot, you know. Half the time they're in hysterics! You should see them nearly bust a gut. They think I'm crazy. Sit down. Let me get you a beer. Let me get dressed.

MIKE

It's a little early for a beer.

MARY

Oh, come on, you're an adult now. You can have a beer with your mother. When'd you get home? Sit down. I'll get you a beer.

MIKE

Last night.

(MARY gets a beer from the refrigerator and returns.)

You went to the doctor? That's good! Who'd you see?

MARY

Dr. Kranishnita. New. Dr. Hughes retired. All the doctors in town are Indians now. Or Filipinos, they say. I told him I have a son in law school. He said I should be very proud! I am! I told Eleanor you were coming home, and she said it'd be good for me. A real boost to my spirits. Oy! You should see what goes on in the street here. I swear, it's like a whorehouse across the street, a whorehouse with kids. Her boyfriends at all hours. I think she's got a boyfriend on all three shifts. I'm afraid to go for groceries. Yeh! I call in. They have a boy deliver. I leave the money outside the door and listen till he's good and gone. Your father's been here. He calls from bars. He comes over and knocks on the door. "Mary… Mary… It's Mike… Let me in…" He passed out on my couch one night. Yeh. Right here, his arm on the floor. Passed out! Snoring! God!

(MARY has not yet passed the beer can to him.)

MIKE

I'm glad you still talk together.

MARY

I haven't seen him in months. Eleanor's daughter's getting married. Elaine. You remember Elaine. Sure. You went to school with her.

MIKE

Oh. Elaine Cassin. Sure! Who's the guy?

MARY

Some guy from Braddock. A nice fella, they say. There's a man in the neighborhood who's after me. He's been to the door. He called me. That's

MARY *(cont.)*
why I won't answer the phone. "Hello, honey." Oh God. That's why I can't go out. I think he'd rape me. I can tell you that, can't I? I think he'd rape me.

MIKE
Sit down, Mom. Relax.

MARY
He's been to the door!

MIKE
Do you know his name? Have you told him to stay away?

MARY
What do you mean, relax? What's wrong with me?

MIKE
Nothing!

MARY
Did you come over to attack me?

MIKE
No! I'm sorry. I didn't mean to upset you. But, uh… where's my beer?

MARY
Oops! Ha!

(MARY gives him the unopened can.)

MIKE
You're nervous, see?

MARY
I can be nervous. I haven't seen you in a long time.

MIKE
Yeh. I'm nervous too. I'm so glad to see you!

MARY

You don't have to be nervous with me. I'm your mother. But I'm not dressed. That could make a man nervous. Look at this robe. I just threw it on. Let me get dressed.

MIKE

I'll get you a beer.

MARY

I just want a little. Just a glass. Sit down. I'll just be a minute. You talk. Don't come over here. You could see me getting dressed. The door doesn't close. Huh! I don't know what's wrong. It must be warped.

MIKE

I'm no carpenter, but I'll look at it.

MARY

Not now, though! It just closes partway.

MIKE

I won't peek.

MARY

What does it matter? I'm just being silly. Talk to me!

(MARY goes into the bedroom. MIKE opens his beer, goes into the kitchen, gets her beer from the refrigerator, washes two glasses and returns.)

MIKE

I'll be in town a few days. Spring break. Maybe we can go out somewhere together.

MARY

(from the bedroom)
Oh no! We can talk here

MIKE

I like to see the landscape: the miles of old mills along the rivers, the hills.

MARY
I think that's ... goofy! You go away to school, study the world, everything, and you like this dump. Why not ... Florida!?

MIKE
This is where I grew up.

(MARY enters from bedroom, wearing a dress and adjusting a wig.)

MARY
And left as soon as you could, regardless.

MIKE
Regardless of what?

MARY
Is my wig on straight?

MIKE
It's ,,, not all the way on.

MARY
That's how it fits. It fits a little funny.

MIKE
That's fine, looks fine.

MARY
And that's why you're home? To see the mills and hills? A dead town?

MIKE
To see you and see Dad. How come the refrigerator's full of beer?

MARY
I got some for you—in case you came over.

MIKE
But there's nothing else, Mom. There's a few slices of cheese-food and some mustard and twenty cans of beer.

MARY

I haven't been shopping.

MIKE

You got the beer.

MARY

I don't feel like eating much, alright? And I've got lots of cans.
I like canned food. It keeps.

MIKE

Want me to go shopping later?

MARY

Would you?

MIKE

Sure.

MARY

That'd be nice. Yeh.

MIKE

Have you been to the doctors?

MARY

Don't pick at me, Mikey, please.

MIKE

It's important.

MARY

It doesn't matter anymore.

MIKE

It could make a difference.

MARY

I don't care anymore, Mikey. I've had cancer for seven years.
And what else do I have? Nothing! These rooms that I hardly ever
leave. I just want to die, finally.

MIKE

No, Mom.

MARY

You don't know what it's like. And people don't care. They don't help. You're the best, Mike. You. I tell people that.

MIKE

I don't do enough. I love you, Mom. A lot of people love you. We all care.

MARY

Then where are they?

MIKE

It's hard. We had a very hard past. It takes time to heal.

MARY

And your brothers?

MIKE

They were younger. They took all that fighting hard.

MARY

Where are they?

MIKE

Dave has a different spring break. I don't think he's coming home, either. And Stevie's in California. That's a long trip.

MARY

Can't people help me?

MIKE

What about your sister—Aunt Judy?

MARY

I don't see why I can't live with Judy. I suggested it to her, and she got mad.

MIKE
She's a single, working woman. Maybe she can't be weighed down.

MARY
Weighed down? I'm not that heavy.

(THEY laugh.)

She yelled at me for drinking whiskey. I don't think whiskey hurts, but she does.

MIKE
People are afraid.

MARY
Of what?

MIKE
Afraid of you! I'm sorry! You hurt us! That's over now, I know, but people are afraid of how much you need now. That's why you have to be strong, always. If you stand on your own some, people will help.

MARY
Why'd you come home? You think I'm dying this time, don't you? I told you not to come. I'm scared now.

(MARY starts to cry.)

MIKE
No, Mom. Hey.

(MIKE embraces her while she cries.)

MARY
You'd only come to see me die.

MIKE
I love you, Mom. No.

MARY
I don't want the doctors. My hair will fall out. This chemotherapy's terrible. I need you, Mikey.

MIKE
I'll do all I can, Mom. I promise.

MARY
How much is that?

MIKE
I think we should go to the doctor together.

(MARY *pulls away.*)

MARY
Let me show you something. You'll love this. Drink your beer. This is so cute. Eleanor won it at a raffle at the Legion. It was a joke prize. She gave it to me. "Just what you need, Mary!" It's a riot. I showed it to the nurses. They were hysterical. Where is it? Drink up! I'll get you another.

MIKE
I've still got some.

MARY
Get another. Go on. You'll love this.

(*MARY goes into the bedroom.*
MIKE goes to the kitchen, gets another beer and returns.
MARY returns with a small plastic doll of a young boy standing facing a fire hydrant.)

MARY
Here it is. Sit down. Look at this.

MIKE
A little boy.

MARY
Now watch. You pull his pants down … and he pees! On the fire hydrant! Look at his bum and he's even got a little thing! Look!

MIKE
How does it work?

MARY

You put a little tinted water in his back. The nurses went wild.

MIKE

Uh-huh.

MARY

What's the matter? You a prude?

MIKE

No, it's great! I'm glad you showed me.

MARY

I thought you'd like it.

MIKE

I do.

MARY

I wanted to make you laugh. No wonder I'm nervous. You look at me with hard eyes.

MIKE

I love you.

MARY

I need you to tell me that.

MIKE

I'm afraid too.

MARY

Are you drinking your beer?

MIKE

Yes, thank you.

(Pause)

What happened to Flo? She was your best friend. How is she?

MARY
I haven't seen her in years. I don't speak to her anymore.

MIKE
What? Why?

MARY
She hurt me, after my operation—after my breast was removed. I can tell you this. She came over one day with Lois, and they laughed at me. They bought new bras for me, a bunch of them. That was nice at first, but then they treated it like a big joke. They stuffed a cup in each of my new bras with handkerchiefs and padding and waved the bras around, laughing, busting a gut. They thought it was so funny.

MIKE
Really?

MARY
I got furious. I went in the kitchen and slammed the door and told them to get out. I was crying.

MIKE
Oh.

MARY
How can anyone laugh that I had surgery and lost my breast?

MIKE
Maybe there was a misunderstanding.

MARY
How? What?

MIKE
I guess she tried too hard to cheer you up.

MARY
It's not funny.

MIKE
She did it badly. Were you all drinking?

MARY

That's no excuse.

MIKE

Did she apologize?

MARY

They left in a huff, like I did something wrong. I cried a lot because of her.

MIKE

Mom, you cried because you had surgery and lost a breast. You're suffering. She came over to help.

MARY

Why are you taking her side against your mother?

MIKE

I'm not! I'm on your side! I just think maybe there was a misunderstanding. It was an attempt to make you smile. She was your friend.

MARY

No more.

MIKE

I bet she apologized.

MARY

Oh sure, but she thought it was my fault I cried. I told them to get out. She called, afterward. I hung up on her.

MIKE

But give her a chance. You and Flo were friends a long time, from before you were married. You worked in the five-and-ten together, right? After high school? You double-dated. You always laughed with her. Some of my best early memories are at their house. I remember crawling under their table and chairs in a game. Quite a thicket of wooden legs, down there. And they had a laundry chute! We kids stuffed clothes in the laundry chute and ran down to the basement, to see they'd landed in a basket. I looked up the chute from the basement at their boy Bobby's grinning face as he tossed more clothes down. You grown-ups were talking and

MIKE *(cont.)*

joking too, you and Flo and Dad and Jack. I was supposed to marry Flo's daughter, Susan.

MARY

What, get married? When?

MIKE

I was four or five. You grown-ups joked that Susan and I would get married. I thought it made sense—we had fun together, our families were close, we went to the same church, she was cute and a little younger. Then Susan toddled into their living room, wearing a bridal veil, her mother's. She carried flowers too. You grown-ups started telling us to kiss and we'd be married. She ran to me, puckering up, and I panicked! I ran, and she chased me with her bridal veil and flowers, and you all laughed so hard together.

MARY

I don't remember that.

MIKE

Well, the point is, we had good times together. Maybe you should call Flo and forgive her. You might have a friend again.

MARY

She won't help me. She has her own family, her own kids. I'll never see her again. Done.

MIKE

That's a shame.

MARY

Yep!
(Pause)
People say I wasn't a good mother. They say I couldn't have been a good mother, because the mother always gets custody of the kids in a divorce, and you kids went with your father. That was your choice. If you didn't want me, I thought, alright.

MIKE

Oh, jeez.

MARY

People shouldn't say I was a bad mother. I always fed you. You always had clean clothes.

MIKE

You didn't want us. You said that many times.

MARY

After the hearing. After you sat in court on your father's side. After that, it was over.

MIKE

You would have sent him to jail on a lie.

MARY

You had no right to turn on me, I was your mother.

MIKE

You hated us.

MARY

I did not.

MIKE

You beat us. You yelled, screamed.

MARY

Your father was drinking all the time. Always at the beer garden. I remember something. I remember the time you tried to protect me from your father, with a little toy bat. Remember that?

MIKE

No…

MARY

And the Reardens were taking you kids from me.

MIKE

They're family.

MARY

You kids were my family! And I couldn't keep you. You didn't love me. You had hard eyes, all of you looked at me so hard. It would make anyone upset.

MIKE

You scared us. Mom.

MARY

I had two thyroid operations, and it came back. Then the radiation. I always had thyroid. So, why did things get worse? Drink your beer. Don't feel sorry for me, I don't. And I was a good mother.

MIKE

Yes. You always fed us.

MARY

Is your father dating anyone?

MIKE

I don't think so. You know how reserved he is, about telling things.

MARY

What about that woman, Jo Ann?

MIKE

I don't think so. That didn't last long.

MARY

No, he didn't love her. I'm the only one he ever loved. He's been the only man in my life. I was a virgin when we got married. I had to read a book about sex. You're grown. I can tell you this. He comes over sometimes.

MIKE

There has to be a lot of feeling there, always.

MARY

We were married eighteen years. I've never said this, but I must have had cancer before the divorce.

MIKE

What do you mean?

MARY

I mean, I must have been sick with cancer before your father divorced me.

MIKE

No one knew that.

MARY

I mean, he cut off his responsibilities.

MIKE

No one knew you had cancer.

MARY

People knew I was sick. He can't just cut off his responsibilities.

(Silence)

I'm glad you're here, Mike. I need to talk with you. Have another beer. Want some nuts?

MIKE

Yeh, sounds good.

(MARY gets up.)

MARY

What do you think of McGillicuddy?

MIKE

What?

MARY

That's what I call him. Looks like I'm pregnant, doesn't it? I tell people I'm pregnant with McGillicuddy.

MIKE

Why McGillicuddy?

MARY

'Cause he's big, dumb and Irish—like his mother! Isn't that something?

MIKE

Yeh.

MARY

They think it's benign. Looks just like I'm pregnant. You're so serious! You're no fun!

MIKE

Bull! We're gonna do the hustle!

MARY

The dance?

MIKE

Yep.

MARY

They talk about it on Johnny Carson. You do it? At parties? Do you go to parties much?

MIKE

Sure.

MARY

Let's see you do it.

MIKE

Then you'll do it. Yes! I'm gonna teach you. Look. It's the simplest dance ever.

(MIKE sings a disco tune and demonstrates the dance.)

That's all it is. Slide-step. Slide-step. Step, step. That's it! It's all in the style.

(MARY tries the dance. MIKE sings and demonstrates.)

MARY

Come on! Dance with your mother!

(THEY dance and blunder about, laughing.)

Oo! That's too much!

(THEY stop.)

We make a good couple.

MIKE

Yeh.

MARY

I tell people, if they see us walking with me on your arm, they'd think we were lovers. They should see us dancing! Do you have a girlfriend?

MIKE

I have some friends, sure. It's mostly focusing on school, right now.

MARY

You're good for me, Mike. I need you around.

MIKE

I'll only be here this week.

MARY

I'll tell you what would really be good for me. If I could live with you, it would be such a boost.

(MIKE is stunned.)

You could help me eat and see the doctors. I'd be strong then. You would really help. I wouldn't be in the way. I'd let you alone. I could cook. I used to always cook for you. I'd stay in my room when you want, but I'd know you were there. It would make my life good. That's what I need, Mike. I don't need little things. I need support. If I could live with you…

MIKE

Where?

MARY
Near school. An apartment. I'd just need a room in your apartment. I could help you. I'd be quiet.

MIKE
No.

MARY
It would help me so much.

MIKE
It wouldn't work. I couldn't do it.

MARY
Why?

MIKE
It's too much strain.

MARY
How is it for me?

MIKE
I'll do as much as I can, Mom. I can't do that yet.

(Silence)

I'm sorry, Mom. Listen. That's the ideal, that we could live together. But we can't do that yet. It's hard enough to talk together. I love you. Very much. And you love me, don't you? Say it once today, for me.

(MARY says nothing.)

MIKE
We'll do what we can. We'll see the doctors. When did you show the nurses the doll?

MARY
December.

MIKE
Four months ago?

MARY
I stopped going when they said I'd die. They said I had six months. I told you not to come. It scares me. You came because I'm dying, didn't you?

MIKE
I came to see you.

MARY
Of course, I love you—but I need help, so what's that to you? You're a hard man, Mike. Like your father.

MIKE
We're all pretty tough by now.

MARY
I'm the toughest. Have some more beer.

MIKE
Alright. You want some?

MARY
I have this.

(MIKE goes to the refrigerator, gets another beer and returns.)

MARY
Do you think it'd help? The doctors?

MIKE
We should find out. Do you have any pain?

MARY
I don't know anymore.

MIKE
Maybe they could give you some pain killers.

MARY
Krishanutti won't give me any more prescriptions.

MIKE
Why?

MARY
It's silly. He thinks that I'd take too many. I don't know why he thinks that.

MIKE
Why does he think that?

MARY
I don't know! I wish I had some. I tell people, I would never commit suicide. I would never do that to you kids' reputation.

MIKE
What a thing to say.

MARY
What?

MIKE
It's not our reputation that matters.

MARY
You want me to die. Is that what you're saying?

MIKE
No! No! No! I want you to live, for yourself.

MARY
For myself, I want to die.

MIKE
Then live for me, because I love you! Not for my reputation.

MARY
There you go again.

MIKE

Live for me. Live for us, for Dan and Steve and Dad and me. And you. Okay?

MARY

You said your father. Do you think he cares?

MIKE

He's been over, hasn't he?

MARY

Not in a long time. Mike, I know what I need. I know what would really help me.

MIKE

What's that?

MARY

I need support.

MIKE

Yeh…

MARY

I need you to do me a favor. I need you to do this. I want you to ask your father to help me. I need his support. I'd be so happy. I'd get better. I still love him, Mike. I could die in peace if he still loves me.

MIKE

I don't want to get caught between you two.

MARY

Mike, you're my son. I need this.

MIKE

You two fought over me, before. You pulled me in the middle and made me choose and choose and choose between you.

MARY

I'm not saying choose.

MIKE

You want me to go to him to ask something he doesn't want, something huge. That's pulling me into the middle, to tell him I side with you, because it would be choosing sides.

MARY

You still side with your father against me.

MIKE

I remember when I was about six. You two were talking in the kitchen. The quiet, steady murmur was so reassuring, so nice, the level flow of your calm voices after nights of terrible yelling. Dad called me into the kitchen. You both sat at the table. And Dad said, "Mike, if your mother and I get a divorce, who would you want to live with, me or her?" Shock! Dumbfounded. And you both watched me squirm. I whined and shook my head and said, "I want both of you, I want both." Then, when you stayed together, I thought it was my fault you were so unhappy.

MARY

You made your choice. You chose your father. Now I'm talking about both, about having us both.

MIKE

Oh Mom.

MARY

It would be both.

MIKE

I don't think I can get caught in the middle.

MARY

It's not a middle. It's both. I asked you once before, in the hospital. Do you remember?

MIKE

Two years ago?

MARY

I asked you to tell your father to visit me in the hospital. That was the worst I ever was. Did you ask him?

MIKE
Yes.

MARY
All you told me was, "I don't know if he'll come." Did you ask him?

MIKE
I even prostrated myself at his feet. I was lying on the floor, going through record albums and looking up and talking as he paused above me, and I suddenly felt I could raise the subject. I told him you were very sick and suggested, very carefully, it might be nice for him to see you. I did, and he just looked down at me, about five feet, and looked very stung. And he walked away.

MARY
That's nothing, Mike. You've got to insist, so he'll listen.

MIKE
He's my father.

MARY
I'm your mother.

MIKE
And I have to choose!

MARY
You did. You chose your father!

MIKE
That's how I survived! I can't go through that again. I can't get in the middle of your marriage and divorce.

MARY
You're part of this family.

MIKE
I can't tell him how to treat his ex-wife. He has a lot of feeling for you, so he has to stay away.

MARY
You'll do this for me, because you chose him. Because you hurt me forever, every day for years, with your sass and your hate.

MIKE
No!

MARY
I need support.

MIKE
You call him. You ask him.

MARY
I can't.

MIKE
But I can?

MARY
For me this once, you can.

MIKE
What's the "support" you want?

MARY
You know.

MIKE
No, I don't.

MARY
He should see me.

MIKE
For my support, you want to live with me.

MARY
No, I don't need that from your father. We live in the same dead town. You know what I need.

MIKE
No.

MARY
I want him to love me.

MIKE
Then what?

MARY
I want him to show it. I just want to know he loves me.

MIKE
I'm not gonna get caught in the middle.

MARY
You said you'd help me, but help isn't little things.

MIKE
You need groceries.

MARY
I can't shop.

MIKE
I'll go get some. I'll be back.

MARY
So soon?

MIKE
I need to go out.

MARY
Let me make a list.

MIKE
I don't need a list. You need everything, except mustard and beer.

MARY
I don't like some things.

MIKE
I'll only get things I like. I'll take them, if you won't.

MARY
Would you get me some whiskey?

MIKE
Sure. What kind?

MARY
Just whiskey. Seagram's. Let me get you money.

MIKE
Don't worry about it. When I get back, we'll work on the doctors. We'll make an appointment. Say, what's this guy look like, who's been bothering you? Maybe I'll see him.

MARY
Oh, don't worry about him. He's just silly, thinks he's a lover man. Mister Smooth! I'll pay you when you get back. Kiss your mother?

(THEY embrace.)

We won't fight. We're through fighting.

*(MIKE exits.
MARY goes to the couch and sits down.)*

BLACKOUT

SCENE 2

SETTING: MIKE'S FATHER'S house. Night. Living room, with sofa, chairs and television. At left, front door. Left rear, stairs to the second floor. A dim hall light is on, and a lamp in the living room.

AT RISE: MIKE comes in the front door. He goes to the living room, turns on another light and sits down.

                BETH
          (offstage, upstairs)

Mike?

                MIKE

Yeh? Hi, Aunt Beth!

    (BETH appears at the top of the stairs. She wears a night gown, robe and slippers.)

                BETH

That's young Mike.

                MIKE

Yeh.

                BETH

I thought that was maybe your father coming in.

    (MIKE goes to the foot of the stairs to speak with her.)

                MIKE

No. I'm back from Dave's. He dropped me off.

                BETH

This isn't like your father lately.

MIKE
What?

BETH
Staying out. I get worried.

MIKE
You shouldn't have to wait up, Aunt Beth. Get your rest.

BETH
Yeh, but I can't help worrying. What are your plans for tomorrow?

MIKE
I thought I'd spend the morning here, then go over and see Mom.

BETH
Again?

MIKE
She needs help, Aunt Beth.

BETH
We all could use help, Mike.

MIKE
She's sick with cancer.

(BETH comes downstairs.)

BETH
I know I shouldn't be the one to talk, Mike. I know what she thinks I did, and I should be the last one to ever say anything against her. But I'm getting worried about you. You're getting too involved. I know she's your mother, Mike, but you don't owe that woman anything.

MIKE
It's not about "owing!" She's my mother!

BETH
She treated you kids like shit. You used to come stay at my place, to get away from her. Sometimes you were really upset, shaken, crying. One

BETH *(cont.)*
time, you were ten. She'd thrown you out of the house, with bus fare. She used to beat on you—with paddles! And slapping! I could tell you an earful, what she did.

MIKE
There's no point.

BETH
No, you listen, Mike. She tried to kill you once, you kids. She turned on all the gas valves in the kitchen. This was when you lived on Harrison Street. She went to bed with you kids asleep and all the gas on. And she left a note, saying that your father had driven her to it. She did. This happened. Your father was working four-to-twelve. But he arranged to get relieved early that night, because he was worried about things. He found the front door latched with the chain—remember, she used to lock him out with the door chain?—and he smelled gas. He got in through a window and turned the gas off and aired the place out and sat up all night figuring what to do next with all your lives. He was lucky to come home early, no, he knew to worry. That's your mother. I'm sorry. We never told you kids that, but it's true.

MIKE
How did he let us spend another night with her?

BETH
He didn't. You kids came over to my place for a few days. You thought it was a treat.

MIKE
I might remember that.

BETH
They talked it out, I guess. It looked like things would be better. You went back. What else do you do? You live with your family.

MIKE
That was her thyroid.

BETH
She was an awful woman.

MIKE
Now she's dying.

BETH
Why do you think she's dying?

MIKE
What?

BETH
Who told you she is? She did.

MIKE
She has cancer, she was hospitalized, had surgery…

BETH
She had cancer. They got it out years ago.

MIKE
That's quite a thing to say.

BETH
When she was in the hospital, a couple years ago, it wasn't cancer. It was malnutrition. She wasn't eating. I'm sorry. I doubt every word that woman ever says. You know very well she lies. God forgive me, if she's dying.

MIKE
I'm trying to get her to the doctor.

BETH
And why won't she go?

MIKE
She's worn out. She's not eating.

BETH
That woman had your father arrested twice, on lies. She tried to put him in jail, in the workhouse in Pittsburgh, for an imaginary assault. She went down to the fire chief and tried to have your father fired. She did. She called him a drunkard and said he beat her, and she asked them to fire

BETH *(cont.)*
him from his job. As if that would have helped anyone! Remember, she used to call here in the middle of the night? That was her, all those phone calls at night.

MIKE
Sure.

BETH
She's still up to no good, Mike. And you're falling for it. I'm sorry, but you are.

MIKE
These are hard words, Aunt Beth. It's not like you.

BETH
God forgive me, but I care about you. I can't let this happen.

MIKE
What?

BETH
Your father's been drinking every night since you said you were coming. And before that, he was so quiet. He was coming home every night, reading the paper, watching TV. I do wish he had a girlfriend. He seems sort of lonely. A man his age shouldn't be alone, it's not natural. But he was alright, till this.

MIKE
He's drinking because I'm home?

BETH
Because you're stirring up matters with your mother. Bless your heart, you're good to care for her, but don't get hurt. You owe yourself to stay away. I have to say this. Your father won't say it. I know your mother. I know what she says about me, that I stole her kids. And I may burn in hell, there's a grain of truth in that.

MIKE
Oh no, Aunt Beth. You helped us so much.

BETH

You were like my kids. I never had my own. I only stepped in, because I had to. You kids were so wrecked by her, so confused and hurt and beaten, it's a miracle you've turned out okay, and by God, I had something to do with that. Yes, I moved into this house just a month after she moved out, because you needed a woman here, with your father working.

MIKE

Yes, yes! Thank you.

BETH

I feel sick to my stomach, talking to you of your own mother this way, but I have to.

MIKE

It's alright. But what I see now is a desperately unhappy woman, who's dying. She's been abandoned over there on Jenny Lind Street, hated, rejected, feared by her own children. I think that one of the few real tasks I have in life is to try to help my mother in her illness. If that makes someone drink, well, get over it!

BETH

What your father went through for you kids…

MIKE

This should be easy.

BETH

He stayed married till you were all old enough that the court wouldn't have to award you to your mother. And that was a long, hard time.

MIKE

Those were awful years.

BETH

So, don't borrow his car to go see her.

MIKE

Okay, I'll take the bus.

BETH

She's using you against him.

MIKE

Why can't I take my mother to the doctor?

BETH

She's using it, even her illness. She would cut herself to pieces to spite us.

MIKE

I think the decent, human way to deal with this is to see her, help her, and for the open, honest reason that I love her, like I love Dad, like I love you. Any tensions from that, we'll just deal with, decently.

BETH

I wish to God you were right. I hope you can help that poor woman. But be careful. And think of your father's feelings.

MIKE

It's about love, the same love that I have for him.

(SOUND of a car pulling up and parking outside.)

BETH

Is that your Dad?

MIKE

Sounds like his car.

BETH

Speak of the devil!

MIKE

I have to help her.

BETH

But be careful!

MIKE

I'm always careful, Aunt Beth. I'm too careful.

BETH

There's no such thing as too careful.

(MIKE'S FATHER can be heard singing to himself softly. He comes in the front door.)

MIKE

Hi, Dad!

BETH

Hello there!

FATHER

How's everybody?

BETH

Just fine, thanks!

MIKE

Fine!

FATHER

I thought you were going out tonight.

MIKE

I just got back.

FATHER

How'd you go?

MIKE

I saw Dave and Larry. Dave gave me a ride.

FATHER

I was wondering.

BETH

You said Mike could have your car tonight.

MIKE

It doesn't matter.

FATHER

That's what I was wondering about. I wasn't sure if I said something.

MIKE

It worked out.

FATHER

If I said that, I'm sorry, Mike. I forgot all about it.

MIKE

Dave gave me a ride.

FATHER

Good. I don't know how I could have forgotten.

BETH

Would you like a sandwich?

FATHER

Nah. Nothing, thanks. Do you need the car tomorrow?

MIKE

Are you working day-turn?

FATHER

Yeh. Take the car.

MIKE

Thank you, but I won't need the car. I'll hang around here, then maybe in the afternoon go over on the bus and see Mom.

(Silence. THE TWO MEN stare at each other.)

BETH

I'll just leave you two to your talk, because I'm going to bed!

FATHER

Good night! Thank you!

MIKE
Thank you!

(BETH goes upstairs and exits.)

FATHER
Go ahead. You can borrow the car. Go visit your mother.

MIKE
I'm just trying to show some support, even a little, in her illness.

FATHER
Yes, that's a good thing. I'm not stopping you. You can have my car.

MIKE
You seem so uneasy.

FATHER
We went through hell with that woman. I put up with it for years, to save you kids. Finally, I could divorce her. Now you go back to her. You carry messages from her, things she tells you, new things she wants. She's trying to take you away.

MIKE
Take me away? I don't even live here. I live hundreds of miles away.

FATHER
I mean with her stories, to put distance between us. I look at you when you return, to see what her next move is.

MIKE
Our love has to be more than a power struggle.

FATHER
"Love!" That's a lot of pain, Mike, around the hope of … being comfortable together, I guess. Things get said. Get done. And you lose comfort, lose hope, once and then again, and again. Sometimes it's better just to let things go. Mary and I loved each other. We met right after the war. We got married right away, had kids, put the war behind us, were normal. Love! We had it, with a mortgage on a small house. We had no privacy, no space. Maybe that was the problem—our little love cottage. We stayed way too long there. We broke up here, after we moved, but it all

went bad back there. You never know! And then you know!

> MIKE

You had no time, either. You worked two jobs!

> FATHER

Love exists in space and time, Mike. Nowhere else. We didn't have enough of either, but that's all we get. Take it easy!

(FATHER sits on the couch.)

People want a lot of things. Good health. Long life. You don't always get what you've paid for.

> MIKE

I remember you sitting on the couch in our old house, one night. Not that couch, the red one. You were drunk and very distant. You were upset. You leaned your head back, then slumped forward, murmuring, "You don't love me, none of you love me." We boys were little and all in our pajamas. We were hugging you and crying. Danny and I kept pleading over and over, "We do love you, we do," while we cried. Stevie was a baby. He was standing on the couch, clutching you. I see Stevie's baby face, all scrunched up eyes and wailing with a wide mouth, scared by all our crying. I was kneeling, hugging your knees. And you kept muttering, "No, you don't love me. You side with your mother. I'll just go away." We were terrified that you'd go.

> FATHER

Your mother was turning you against me, even the baby. Not letting you talk to me… Not even letting you give me Christmas cards!

> MIKE

We hand-made cards and slipped them to you, as you went to the bathroom.

> FATHER

I was very touched. And very sad. What a life. But I never left you.

> MIKE

Thank you.

FATHER

Lots of fathers do, you know, leave their families.

MIKE

Yes, thank you.

FATHER

I never once left.

MIKE

Right.

FATHER

Every night, back home into that. We all cried that night, right? You said I cried.

MIKE

Yes. And you stayed.

FATHER

I was young too, crying on that couch. What, thirty-two, thirty-three? With three kids and an angry wife. I was trapped. You belonged there, when your old man cried for love. I cried with my children. You persuaded me, hugging me, you saved me. That was enough love for my lifetime.

MIKE

I'll bet we can give more.

FATHER

That would be nice.

(Pause)

MIKE

So, what have you been doing tonight?

FATHER

Now?

MIKE
Yeh.

FATHER
Whoa. Listen to you. Where've I been?

MIKE
I'm just talking.

FATHER
Out! Seeing people!

MIKE
Were you at the beer garden?

(FATHER gets up from the couch.)

MIKE
There was more to the problem. You were away for a lot more time than even your two jobs took. And I know how much of the plumbing job time was spent in the beer joint—when I helped you, I often sat at a table in a bar, eating a fish sandwich and pink pistachios, while you talked baseball at the bar. Other times, Mom would say, "I hear your father's truck is parked outside the Oak Tavern again. I guess he won't be home for dinner." You left us over and over again.

FATHER
Well… It was hard to come home. Sometimes she latched the door, with the chain. Remember me calling through the slightly opened door, "Mikey, Mikey, come open the latch."

MIKE
And I did open it, choosing you right in front of Mom.

FATHER
Thank you.

MIKE
Now I wonder, was that wrong? Was she simply, rightfully afraid of you? Physically? And I let you in?

FATHER
Nothing happened.

MIKE
Not that night. Mom's big grievance was your drinking. You were drunk, she said.

FATHER
Men go to the beer garden after work! They have a few drinks, talk.

MIKE
We kids always excused you. You were just drinking like men do, in a neighborhood bar. Sometimes you had too much. So? We said, "Of course he drinks and stays away. Look at what she does, every time he comes home."

FATHER
Thank you.

MIKE
It's called denial. You did drink a lot. You often were drunk.

FATHER
Those were hard years with your mother, Mike.

MIKE
When we heard your truck rattling home at night, long after dinnertime, we were scared of trouble about to burst wild. There was suspense, as your truck door slammed shut. Maybe you coughed in the street, your footsteps on the porch, then you came in the door with the stink of beer. Mom started right in on your drinking and lateness and missing dinner and spending the grocery money and leaving her alone with the kids. Things get said, that's for sure.

FATHER
I heard all that, lots of times.

MIKE
We sided with you. We were afraid of her. She was arbitrary and cruel.

She screamed a lot. We yearned for your calming attention. And so did she, I'm sure, for the man who wasn't there, who was out getting drunk.

FATHER

What do you think I felt, trying to come home to face more of that? For her to shout and scream for all the neighbors to hear. What a hell house.

MIKE

Then you stormed back out to your truck. You went back to the beer joint. You drank more, came home very late, passed out. And you were our security, you had the job. That was the good guy in the crisis, our Dad.

FATHER

You can't talk this way to me. I raised you. I got you through that. I got custody in the divorce. You were safe, in a calm and quiet place. Here!

MIKE

Please, I don't mean to blame.

FATHER

It sure sounds like it.

MIKE

I want to recognize what happened, what we did, what we're doing now. We can't just blame Mom. Hell, she was in a terrible situation too. We all failed. Even we kids failed, we couldn't help at all. I've got lots of faults. Dad, I have a similar problem Or, it's not really a problem. Same thing as booze, problem, no problem, only with marijuana. I smoke it a fair amount.

FATHER

Oh dear.

MIKE

I have problems too.

FATHER

That's supposed to make it all better? "You were an awful drunk, Dad, but that's okay, because I'm a dope fiend?"

MIKE

Shh! Aunt Beth will hear!

FATHER

If she knew that, she would never sleep a wink again.

MIKE

These dependencies, addictions, can run in families.

FATHER

What, it's my fault you smoke dope?

MIKE

No! I can learn from you, how to do better. Because you got better!

FATHER

It's funny. A part of me is glad. You're so wrapped up in studies, bookish and all that, and that's fine, but it's kinda nice to know you're doing something "hip." You got a little of the old man in you. Not that I'm hip, but I'm…

MIKE

Troubled? Recovered?

FATHER

I do things I like. Well, you're away at school, you're doing "the thing." You're part of the crowd. It's funny, I feel better about that. But just because "everybody's doing it," doesn't mean you have to do it. People get into trouble that way, doing what everybody else does, following "the gang." When you get in trouble, the gang won't be there. They don't want your troubles. Marijuana's illegal. It can ruin your career—you're going to be a lawyer!

MIKE

I'm careful.

FATHER

Famous last words. They say marijuana can lead to harder stuff.

MIKE

It doesn't.

FATHER

Well, I'm sure young people have all the answers. All of history doesn't matter. The law doesn't matter.

MIKE

I don't take any other drug.

FATHER

Well, you know why they've always called it "dope?" I hear kids get all dopey and do goofy things on dope.

MIKE

Hey, I get high and listen to records.

FATHER

Mike, you gotta make your way. I know you're not starting out with all the advantages. You don't need to get dopey too.

MIKE

So, what do I do, Dad?

FATHER

I hear grass smells really bad, kind of sickly sweet. Your neighbors can smell it.

MIKE

Booze stinks.

FATHER

Yeah. But alcohol's legal.

MIKE

I'm glad I can talk about it with you. A lot of people couldn't tell their father.

FATHER

I do try.

MIKE
I know, when we lived with Mom, you had a lot to deal with.

FATHER
I guess that's right.

MIKE
Meaning what, Mom was ill? Yes. That made her difficult. You couldn't help her, couldn't cope, because you were drunk! And that terrified her!

FATHER
Couldn't help? You don't even know about all we did. Did you realize she had surgery twice, for her thyroid? We kept it from you, because we didn't want to scare you. So, you don't even know how I tried.

MIKE
She was full of adrenalin, in fear and fighting mode. She needed reassurance, affection, attention.

FATHER
Oh, you know so much, do you?

MIKE
I'm sure she needed more than she got from you. Yes, she was desperate, ready to scream, by the time you got home at night, drunk.

FATHER
You want to argue? Is that what you want? Because I can argue!

MIKE
I know! I remember!

FATHER
You're sounding just like your mother! Why can't I have a little peace, when I get home? Then things will be fine! But no, I have to get an earful of yakking! I'm better off at the beer garden. You know what they yak about—sports! And it's always the player's fault, or the manager's, not mine!

BETH

(from offstage, upstairs)
What's the problem down there?

FATHER
It's okay, Beth!

(BETH appears at the top of the stairs.)

BETH
It doesn't sound okay. How's a body to sleep?

FATHER
Mike and I got some things to talk about. We'll keep it down.

BETH
Please do. Talk nicely. Mike, I mean young Mike. Look what you're doing here. I warned you.

MIKE
Yes.

BETH
Not to get things riled up.

MIKE
We're having a good talk.

BETH
Good night, then.

(BETH exits upstairs.)

FATHER
Where were we?

MIKE
Illness.

FATHER
I'm not sick a day in my life, well, except when my back slips out.

MIKE
That's from the war, isn't it? When your plane was shot down?

FATHER
Yeh, I think it started with that. Whole damn plane hit smack on the big ocean. Then I had to scramble out and swim! Some buddies drowned, floundering in a whole ocean. Just lost sight of them. Sorry—never talk about that. Right after the war, you bring up these terrible, haunting things you went through, and right away, guys tell you, ahh, shut up, no one wants to hear that, everyone's got a story. So you shut up.

MIKE
How's your back?

FATHER
It's fine, thanks. Good for a long time. I'm not sick, I do manual labor. I do like peace and quiet. Mary and I didn't have peace and quiet much. Not for long. We argued. She was sick with thyroid and I drank, I guess. But you see how I drink. If no one's yelling at me, I get quiet.

MIKE
You doze, slow and distant. Sometimes you mutter sullen, embittered things…

FATHER
What do I say?

MIKE
Oh, life's disappointing, don't count on people…

FATHER
The truth from your father.

MIKE
Then you pass out.

FATHER
Right. I'm quiet. I'm not overbearing, I'm not mean. I did drink too much sometimes, like lots of men in this town. So, why didn't Mary just welcome me home? Let me settle down a moment, rest on the couch, talk a little. Then I would have come home.

MIKE
You're asking me to answer that?

FATHER
No. I guess the drinking—and the money drinking cost—worried her.

MIKE
And your absence.

FATHER
I knew everything she was screaming was true. But why did she have to scream it? That's hard on the ears, it hurts. We've all made mistakes, Mike. Mary and I made big mistakes together. Me especially, probably, for sure. I can't deny it. We can't go back and fix things. You just go ahead with your life and don't look back like this. You'll get all twisted in so many loose ends, and you'll be finding, "Ooo, maybe this is connected to that," or, "Ooo, maybe this means the opposite… and what really happened… Ooo…" Where will it get you? Nowhere. You're letting Mary twist you around. You sided with me, a long time ago. Right choice.

MIKE
I still feel responsibility toward my mother.

FATHER
Of course, and that's a great thing. But keep it in perspective. I'm just gonna read the obituaries.

(FATHER sits with the newspaper. Soon he looks up.)

Let me tell you something about doctors, Mike. We did everything the doctors told us to do. Mary had all that surgery. When the swelling still came back in her neck, her thyroid, we went like the doctors said to the research center for radiation treatment. I drove her down to Pittsburgh several times, where they shot doses of radiation into her neck. No wonder she got cancer, huh? And the doctors never said anything about my drinking. If there was a connection, if it would have helped Mary, maybe I'd have stopped.

MIKE
Yes. Yes, you would have.

FATHER

So that's that.

MIKE

Yes.

FATHER

Well, let's see who's died.

MIKE

I was thinking out loud, Dad, sharing with you. It's good to work things through together, right?

FATHER

If you have to get something off your chest, sure. We're done with it, right?

MIKE

I'm afraid I've hurt your feelings.

FATHER

Nah.

MIKE

That's one of my worst fears—that I might hurt your feelings. As if feelings aren't hurt and mended all the time in family. I'm afraid any hurt to you would be enormous. You'd hide your hurt. I wouldn't even know.

FATHER

I'll let you know.

MIKE

Maybe I'd slowly realize, if you were sulking. Are you sulking?

FATHER

No, Mike. I'm moving on to the next thing. I want to read the paper. You had to get something off your chest, about me drinking and you smoking marijuana. We had our little father-son talk about drugs and drinking, like they say to, on TV.

MIKE

Thanks, Dad!

FATHER

Hey, maybe the drug's got your mind working this way, Mike, all this remembering and wondering. It makes problems for you. You got school to think about, and the future, not the past. It's not your fault. You were just a kid. And I'm not gonna say it's my fault or anyone else's. It's not Mary's fault, poor woman, she was sick. Just let it alone now. It's the best way.

(FADE TO BLACK.)

*(FATHER exits in the dark.
MIKE steps forward into a SPOTLIGHT.)*

MIKE

Well, I phoned my mother, but she wouldn't go to the doctor.

*(MARY enters and joins MIKE in the spotlight.
She is better dressed than previously.)*

MARY

Support wasn't about going to a doctor once. That was just a gesture you made up. I was on a waiting list for more chemotherapy, nothing to be done but wait. I had my doctors. I wanted a son.

MIKE

I couldn't live with you.

MARY

You did, for sixteen years.

(LIGHTS COME UP again on the living room.)

I lived here, a while, what, two years? We finally moved out of that tiny house as you boys got so big. And I got involved in PTA, remember? I volunteered. I was legislative secretary for the PTA. I wrote to Harrisburg and got lots of information about proposed laws. I had a desk in the hallway.

MIKE
Right there. Piled with thick manila packets from the capital.

MARY
A lot of it was about civil rights. And I cheered for civil rights marches and Martin Luther King, because he was for freedom. You saw it with me, I think—the "I have a dream" speech on TV. I stood for the speech, calling out, "Go, Martin!" and "You tell 'em!"

MIKE
Yes. I remember.

MARY
I was fighting too, for freedom from a man, from a drunk.

MIKE
You were a new person.

MARY
I was gonna be a new person, until I got sick. This was my house. I fought over every foot of this place. But I fooled you all. I left all at once, one day with a moving van, while your dad was at work and you kids were at school. I separated. Surprise!

MIKE
I came home from school to find the furniture gone! I went from bare room to room, taking out the storm windows and letting in the air. It was spring. The breeze felt liberating. You were gone!

MARY
No address, no phone number, not one word for any of you, just gone! And I got a job!

MIKE
And then you'd call at night, ringing and ringing. I'd answer and get silence, long silence.

MARY
I don't know what calls you got.

MIKE

I started telling you about my day, into the silence. Urged you to speak. Silence. I'd hang up. Minutes later, another call, ringing and ringing.

(MARY exits.)

MIKE

She moved out seven years ago. Divorce followed. And after visiting her this spring break, and not agreeing to have her live with me, I went back to law school. I called her, a few times. Sometimes she sounded scared. She always wanted comfort, reassurance I tried to give, within such narrow bounds. Then I had a summer job in New York and lived with my girlfriend. What a summer, a city, a woman! Busy days and sultry nights. I let my calls lapse. Mom didn't have my new phone number. In August, I got a call.

FATHER
(offstage)
I got bad news, Mike. Real bad. Your mother passed away.

MIKE

Oh no.

FATHER
(offstage)
A neighbor found her today. She died in bed.

MIKE

Passed away in her sleep?

FATHER
(offstage)
I hope so.

MIKE

I'll be home as fast as I can.

FATHER
(offstage)
She left a note. She wanted Bidler's funeral home. Probably the funeral's on Thursday.

MIKE

She died alone?

(Silence)

MIKE

How long is it, since I talked to her? Two months? She said I was her support. I gave her courage. I feel like thin skin wrapped over a block of lead.

I learn, the doctor declined to fill in a cause of death, on the death certificate. He wasn't sure she'd died of cancer. The coroner wants to do an autopsy. My brothers and I are next of kin. We consent.

Taped to her bedroom mirror was a note with instructions for her funeral and an obituary she'd written for herself. Well, she'd prepared for death. She lived with the note up there,

I guess, ready to be found. Or was it a suicide note, empty of emotions? Did she overdose some medicine? No, the doctor had her off medications, because he was afraid she'd kill herself…

It was glossed over. The coroner's note came the morning of the funeral. In the space for cause of death, it said, "liver failure." That could be a drug overdose, right? Something was kept quiet under those words.

Suicide was a rational way out of suffering. But to choose it, do it, alone! I guess they do. She couldn't even find me!

There are few real obligations in life, or maybe that's just what I think. There are so many obligations, but none I notice. I failed a big one.

A coffin to carry, so light, and the body shifting. Flowers heaped at a hole.

We go to her apartment. Her closets are piled with pill bottles. She saved the empty vials? And beer cans. Empty whiskey bottles are buried like big prizes packed among the vials and cans. And my letters from college, in a box. I throw them out.

I return to school, and my brothers finish the job, place a classified ad and sell her furniture right away to a young couple, give her clothes to Goodwill, vacate the apartment, erase her place.

I expect nothing from relationships, because I have so little to give.

On the morning of Mom's funeral, I dreamed an alarm was clamoring in her open grave. From the grave, the noise was loud, insistent, eternal, beside me but far out of reach and I didn't reach.

(MARY *enters, in her better clothes.*)

MARY
I lay dreaming of my mother and dad holding me. They stroked my hair. I climbed on them. I was a loved little child. You never knew them. They died when I was… a child. They loved me. They were so much comfort at the end, more welcoming than anyone else ever gave me. I could feel them lying side by side with their arms reaching out to me, to lie down with them now. You think you figured in my dying nights, and you did, but I was remembering my own Mom, who died young. Hers was the comfort I missed, every day. I wasn't scared of my mother. Better to be with her than with the strangers who were my husband and children. Strangers, who took the meals I made and gave and glared and scoffed at my sickness and left me!

MIKE
I have so little to give. I'm sorry.

MARY
I won't say love in your father's house. Not in this house, where we screamed our glad good-riddance at each other. We laid a curse on each other here.

MIKE *walks off.*

After I left, right away, your Aunt Beth was here, taking my place. You get back here!

MIKE
(offstage)
What?

MARY
I'm not done with you. Get in here!

(MIKE re-enters.)

MIKE

What?

MARY

When you were little, in the little house on Harrison Street, your father and I had a few quiet moments, when we tried to talk together, fix things. But you kids were yakking in bed! We had no privacy, and I got so mad because your fooling around talking instead of sleeping was ruining my life, my last chance, right then. I was frantic for a chance at peace—yes, the chance for sex too. You kids gave me no rest, even at night.

MIKE

We were just talking.

MARY

And your father and I were trying to talk! To save my marriage and my life! I rushed into your bedroom right to your beds, saying…

(MARY comes at MIKE, raising her arm to strike.)

If you kids don't shut up in here…. I said BE QUIET!

*(MARY slaps him.
MIKE ducks behind the couch.
MARY bends and slaps, like a mother slapping a child in bed, repeatedly. The impact is unseen.)*

Go to sleep, or I'll be back in here. Don't turn away from me, get over here.

(MARY slaps again.)

MIKE

I'm sorry. I'll be good. Don't hit me.

MARY

I'll be back in here, if I hear one more peep.

(MARY steps away.)

MARY *(cont.)*
Well, that spoiled the mood. Your dad didn't like that. Maybe that ended our chance. You ruined my life right then, carrying on and yakking in bed.

(MARY comes at him again, slapping.)

You kids gave us no peace!

*(MARY exits.
(After she has gone, MIKE re-emerges.)*

MIKE
Ah, the domestic violence, at last coming out. And not only standard child-rearing discipline of the time, with paddles, but veering off-track with fits of rage. Did I ever tell you about the dog-and-bird act?

What could be more romantic
than my mother playing
Johnny Matthis constantly?

Then Dad, drunk in his
plumbing clothes (jeans and a work shirt),
surrounded by beer breath,
opened the cage in the dining room.

Dad scared out Mom's pet
parakeet, pretty Dickybird,
in a wild night at our house.

The green bird fluttered to
the mantel while
Dad taunted the dog.
"Get the birdie! Come on!"

The dog barked excitement.
Dad pushed the bird from

the knick-knacks on the mantel.
The tame bird hopped to the rug.

                    MIKE *(cont.)*

"Get the birdie! Come on!"
We boys cried, "No!"
together in the living room.
The bird hopped again,
couldn't fly, and
all our family ran shouting.

Then the black dog pounced
on the bird on the rug.

The young dog strutted
with Mom's pet in its teeth.
"Grr Grr," sang the proud dog
of its kill. Boy, was
Dickie stiff and green
in Roscoe's mouth,
in our black dog's head-
shaking, high-stepping prance of
triumph through the house.

Dad chuckled and sighed,
red-faced, weary on the floor.
Mom cried in the kitchen,
after the screaming and
chase through the house.
                    (Pause)

Then there was the time Mom scratched my arm, enough for blood to flow. Dad saw the blood and went to her and shoved her. She fell to a cushioned armchair and off it to the floor, dress askew. Oh, I felt guilty about that. Dad knocked Mom down, because I complained about a little blood.

Then there was the time she claimed he hit her. She was telling everyone, and going out to bowling league with a large, green, apparent bruise under her left eye. First, she showed it to me. I told her frankly that it looked like make-up, and she turned away. My bias? My state of denial? I don't know, but I was pretty sure it was fake, then.

MIKE (*cont.*)

I'm sure I didn't want to recognize it, if it was true. Two incidents, at least, happened—parakeet and pushing. So, what do I know? What can I ever know or do, from such a base beginning?

(MIKE exits.)

BLACKOUT

Scene 3

SETTING: The living room of FATHER'S house, twenty-four years later. It is a memory landscape, and nothing has changed.

AT RISE: LIGHTS COME UP on full stage again.

OLDER MIKE comes downstairs, as if FATHER is emerging from freshening up and changing clothes. OLDER MIKE is the same actor who plays FATHER. He is dressed like a middle-class professional at his ease in 1996. By the time he is downstairs, he has lost his bearings.

OLDER MIKE

Today I walked to the ironmaster's shop,
Mender of beds broken—
A deep garage, the sharp dust of cuttings,
The metal tang of copper and iron
And that old smell... the odor of Go-Jo solvent,
An oil gel, a salve to wash hands & forearms
Of pipe & grime. Benzene? My madeleine,
A roughed-in doorframe...

My father's hands
Glistening in Go-Jo
Scooped from a canister,
Clasped in cleaning,
The dirt sliding away,
And now my hands too,
Turning in the basement.
The furnace and hot water heater
Enclose us, the floor beams cover us.
The pilot light is steady as the threat of hell.

Joined in work together, a job done, maybe
We'll have a pleasant dinner with Mom
Upstairs in the kitchen, footfalls overhead.

What next? Did we, as we sometimes did,
Talk quietly and laugh around the table,
In that one night of thirty years,
Or did someone go wrong, someone drive off?

(MARY enters, still in her better clothes.)

MARY

Mike?

OLDER MIKE

Young Mike.

MARY

I fell in love with a young Mike.

OLDER MIKE

How are you with older Mikes?

MARY

Just so-so. At best. You look and sound like your Dad!

OLDER MIKE

But I'm slimmer, right, maybe?

MARY

It was a compliment.

OLDER MIKE

I do a lot less drinking, but a lot less physical labor too.

MARY

You're no better.

OLDER MIKE

I'm not better than Dad, no way. I'm just skinnier, maybe, a little. But I have so many of his mannerisms. I stand with my hands in my pockets and say, "all set?"

MARY

I know that one.

OLDER MIKE
I have his reserve, his silence.

MARY
I sure know that one. Sit down. Make yourself at home.

OLDER MIKE
This was our home.

MARY
Briefly. Have a few drinks. Get sullen and bitter, then speak up!

(MARY and OLDER MIKE sit on the couch.)

OLDER MIKE
My voice has a hard edge, it seems, just like the old man's. Apparently, my voice hurts women. And my eyes, and the set of my jaw. It's not even what I say. It's the look on my face. It's my silence. So I'm told! And told! Oh, and I did learn to shout! It just roars out of me suddenly. I'm being emphatic, I think, not yelling, but there I am, loud and angry. Looks and sounds like shouting. Scary. I always apologize. I hate my own yelling.

MARY
Where'd you learn that?

OLDER MIKE
At home! It's where I learned to get yelled at too, and absorbed life with women. Would you believe, I'm attracted to women with your eyes and hair color, women who are nervous or troubled—when it's expressed as artistic temperament. I got married less than a year after you died. And when things went wrong, slowly, and the arguments came and then the yelling, the screaming at me, I realized I'd married my mother. Of course.

MARY
How'd that go?

OLDER MIKE
Divorce, of course. It wasn't fair. I saw you in her, instead of simply her. Would you believe, I wasn't ready for marriage? Couldn't cope with conflict. Every quarrel echoed with scenes of childhood trauma. And I would not be trapped in a bad marriage, like my parents were. I would

OLDER MIKE *(cont.)*

escape through divorce, like you and Dad finally did. Divorce, our great freedom! Thank you, John Milton! For us, there was no counselling, no communication workshops, doing better, making changes, really being committed. No, there were too many echoes of madness in our quarrels. Mine!

MARY

Any children?

OLDER MIKE

Not that time. But my second marriage gave us two children, two girls!

MARY

Great! I wanted a girl.

OLDER MIKE

Now they're children of divorce, my second. But they're doing well. School, sports, friends.

MARY

How old are they? What are their names? Do you have pictures?

(OLDER MIKE pulls snapshots from his wallet and gives them to MARY.)

OLDER MIKE

Rose. And Elizabeth.

MARY

They're beautiful! And your brothers?

OLDER MIKE

They're fine too, I think. So far as I know. We're not close. Not that I'd been a protective older brother, but leaving for college, leaving them behind, clinched it—I was not. Later, they both moved West, to different states. We were dispersed. Only rare phone calls, holiday greeting cards pass between us.

MARY

Come on! Married? Kids?

OLDER MIKE
They've both got wonderful wives, I believe. Dan adopted his second wife's kids—two boys. He's active in politics in Colorado. Steve's really big in finance, lives in Houston. His wife works on the boards of charities. Two kids.

MARY
And your father? Whatever happened to him?

OLDER MIKE
He stopped drinking, again, and married a lovely woman from Duquesne. I heard from her. They were hosting their first Thanksgiving together, all her family gathered here. He was hours late from work, showed up drunk in his uniform and stood over all his new in-laws, assembled around the table, waiting and hungry, and proceeded to sneer and stagger and tell them all off. Ruined the holiday and the marriage, all in one swoop.

MARY
See?

OLDER MIKE
And, on his own, he stopped drinking again and found another nice woman. They've been living here happily for years, sharing coffee and the newspaper and television.

MARY
But...

OLDER MIKE
No buts.

MARY
I'm happy for him.
(Pause)

OLDER MIKE
I felt so guilty for so long, about not taking you in to care for you, while you were dying. But it was too much for me!

MARY
You have no idea how much. What did the coroner say I died of?

OLDER MIKE

Liver failure. That's the abdominal cancer. The "benign" tumor, metastasizing.

MARY

Liver failure can be drinking to death. That's what they covered up, not suicide, you dope, but drink, the evidence you wouldn't see, the coroner's notes about beer cans and whiskey bottles at the deathbed. You didn't want to see those, in the bedroom.

OLDER MIKE

Well, the doctor wouldn't give you medication…

MARY

You were amazed at all the beer in the refrigerator. You thought I was a little loony, to have all that beer and no food? Honey, I was thirsty. That was my self-treatment.

OLDER MIKE

You were sober when I saw you.

MARY

That was morning!

OLDER MIKE

You're just saying this, as if it makes me feel better.

MARY

You look back to those all those silent, late night, ever-ringing phone calls that, yes, I made, after I moved out… That was drunk-dialing! I couldn't talk. I'd have slurred my words and been silly. But I missed you!

OLDER MIKE

You wanted to torment us, with the calls.

MARY

I wanted you to remember me.

OLDER MIKE

I do.

MARY

There's no way you could have lived with me. You'd have been overwhelmed by my thirst and need. You would have been exhausted. You can talk about reconciliation, but time is so short. While you're thinking about it, it's already too late. At least you can dream of reconciliation while you die. I did. It's all we have. And we do have it. The dream is real. I was reconciled in my heart, to all of you. I raised three boys. I'm your mother. Listen to me.

THE END

William Considine writes poems and plays. He was born in McKeesport, PA. He obtained higher education on scholarships and work-study. He graduated "With Great Distinction" from Stanford and cum laude from Harvard Law School. He was first encouraged to write poetry by Diane Middlebrook and first studied writing poetry with Elizabeth Bishop.

Bill was a member of the playwrights workshop of the New York Shakespeare Festival Public Theater, coordinated by Ed Bullins, with four staged readings there. He had play performances at Theater for the New City, La Mama, Brooklyn Army Terminal, Limbo Lounge, Ear Inn, ABC No Rio and Dixon Place. His video of his long poem "Lincoln in Queens" won the Hometown USA Award from the National Federation of Local Cable Programmers in 1990, for excellence in video art produced on public access facilities.

His books include *Strange Coherence* (The Operating System 2013), *The Furies* (The Operating System 2017), *The Other Myrtle* (Finishing Line Press 2021), and *Continent of Fire* (Kelsay Books 2022). A CD of poems with music, *An Early Spring*, was released by Fast Speaking Music in 2013. His full-length verse play *The Mysteries* had a staged reading at Polaris North, in New York City, and is being published in 2025 by Spuyten Duyvil. He is a member of the Dramatists Guild, the Polaris North theater artists cooperative, and Brevitas, a poets' cooperative.

He retired as a lawyer and lives with his wife in the New York City area and in Mexico. They have two grown daughters. For more, please see his website, www.williamconsidine.com.

www.ingramcontent.com/pod-product-compliance
Lightning Source LLC
Chambersburg PA
CBHW030058170426
43197CB00010B/1570